Extended Family

LINDA CHASE grew up on Long Island in commuting distance from New York City. She has been a stage costume designer, a Tai Chi teacher and, more recently, a teacher of poetry and creative writing. Her first collection, *These Goodbyes*, was published by Fatchance Press in 1995. She is a part-time tutor on the MA course at Manchester Metropolitan University and the coordinator of the Poetry School Manchester. She also hosts performance events under the banner Poets and Players to showcase new writers.

Also by Linda Chase from Carcanet Press

The Wedding Spy

LINDA CHASE

Extended Family

CARCANET

Acknowledgements

Some of the poems in this collection were first published in the following magazines: *Envoi, The Frogmore Papers, The North, Parameter, PN Review, The Rialto* and *Tears in the Fence*. A version of 'Younger Men Have Birthdays Too' was published in *PN Review*.

Thanks to Jenifer Giannako and her daughters, Anastasia St. Amand Williams, Michael Arnold, Jemma Kennedy and all those who have shared the house at 163 over the past twenty-five years.

First published in Great Britain in 2006 by
Carcanet Press Limited
Alliance House
Cross Street
Manchester M2 7AQ

A CIP catalogue record for this book is available from the British Library
ISBN 1 85754 867 1
978 1 85754 867 9

The publisher acknowledges financial assistance from Arts Council England

Typeset by XL Publishing Services, Tiverton
Printed and bound in England by SRP Ltd, Exeter

Contents

I Extended Family

Independence	3
The Handover	4
Grand Central Station, 1947	5
The Long Island School (*for Dore Ashton*)	6
The Long Island School (*for Lilian Ruben*)	7
Copley Pond	8
Catching for America	10
The Geography of Goodbyes	11
Launching from Brooklyn	12
Night Light	13
The Last Sane Thing	14
Flights from China	15
Death in the Family	16
Flower Market with My Son	17
3lb 6oz	18
Extended Family	19
Against a Backdrop of Fireworks	20
Tuning Your Cello	21
The Things You Bring	22
Telling You	23
Death Notice	24
Do You Think the Snow Will Stick?	25
Frames of Mind	
1 A Short History of Restraint	26
2 Dead Lock	28
3 Havoc	29
4 The Weeping House	30
5 Two a Day	31
6 Water's Way	32
7 Disarmed	33
8 Cheetham Hill to Crumpsall	34
9 Home Life	35
Keeping the Boys Home	36
Paces	37
Cellar Dance	38
Sharing	39
Premature	40
Nice	41

All Day Goodbyes
  1 Morning Goodbye   42
  2 Afternoon Goodbye   42
  3 Evening Goodbye   43
Confidence   44
Scene Shift   45
One of Them   46
Judo Mad   47
'It's Only Time'   48
The Young Taoist Transcends His Body   49
Passing   50
White China Bowl   50
Consultant   51
The Widow Puts Off Grief   52
Limits   53
Soup Course   54
Immaculate Mother   55
An Amusing Little Breakfast   56
Pre-Op   57
Verse Vampire   58
The Good Sister and the Good Brother   59
Beach Story   60
The Giveaway   61
Upgraded   61
Mentor   62
My Last Lover   63
Still Things Left   64

II   *Younger Men Have Birthdays Too*
Younger Men Have Birthdays Too   67
Love Watch   68
Gamble   69
Loving Parents   70
Purification   71
Secret   72
Restaurant   73
Urgency   74
Cooking for You   75
Journeys with my Phantom Lover   76
Flying to Spain   77
Tuscany   78
The Same as What?   79
Red Wings   80

My Brave Pink   81
Ourselves   82
The Radio Next Door Is Far Too Loud   83
You Have a Daughter   84
Carrot Wheels   85
The GUM Clinic
    1 Sex Talk at the GUM Clinic   86
    2 Prescribed Non-Restrictions   86
    3 Wish You Were Here   87
The Ticking Son   88
Passing the Parcel   89
The Afternoon After   90
The Badly-Done-By Finish   91
The Tin Dragon Fights Back   92
My Friend Who Works   93
Scuffing   94
Out of the Loop   95
Single Was Swell   96
Poetic Licence   97
Early Train South   98
Graffiti   99
Here Again   100
Last Logging On   101
Hacker   102
Dreaming Knows   103
Slow Pink   104

With love,
to my extended family

I
Extended Family

Independence

I'm never in America
on the Fourth of July
but I light a match
and throw it up into the air.

Some years, the ones
in which I feel
intensely patriotic,
I wait till it gets dark.

The Handover

She lowered me into your arms,
your confident, sturdy, two-year-old arms,
like a gift from a guilty weekend,
assuming you'd know what to do with me.
Our father let the handover happen.
Our mother had fallen in love with you
and this was her way of putting things right.
Who knows, she might have killed for you,
but then a baby makes such a good gift.

You taught me everything you knew –
the toddler things like walking, talking, scooting,
then later things like secret forts in woods
and brooks with turtles, ticks and water snakes,
then on to caps and guns and cherry bombs.
I was learning well exactly how to be a boy.

In the mornings, after you woke me up,
I put on swimming trunks without a top
and dived straight into the lake from the tower.
Afternoons, on the hillside trail,
I wore cowboy boots, a neckerchief,
and galloped my horse down the river bed.

Evenings, left by myself in the house,
I wondered if I was perfect.
I know I was perfect for a while.
I remember your face at the door of our den
as you pushed aside a heavy branch
to keep the bad guys out and let me in.

Grand Central Station, 1947

As we got off the train
hand in hand, hot air thick with soot
gusted up, whipping us from behind
and we were caught in a wind tunnel
the length of platform 17.

It propelled us toward anyone
waiting to meet this train at the barrier.
I held on to you, my coupling.
The gate was ahead and we didn't have
the weight to hold us back.

The Long Island School

for Dore Ashton

Underground,
(below her mother's cubist house
wedged within skewed hedges,
so overgrown, so wild their right angles were all but lost)
the art teacher told the children to forget what is real.

The bathroom in her mother's house
was big enough for a phantom horse to enter easily
(after clattering up the central stairs of solid oak)
and then die after first arranging itself in the tub.
'What's new?' her mother would ask. A dead horse in the bathtub.

Her mother's shambled house
(left over from an ideal childhood on Long Island)
was perfect with its sprawling basement, porcelain laundry tubs,
rumbling furnace, fuse boxes, ice skates, boots and sleds.
She could wash brushes, mix paint, wet the clay.

Forget what is real?
(The rent and heat in the city were not abstract.)
Guston, Pollock, Rivers, Rothko were her friends.
She went to their studios, had opinions about their work.
Could her Saturday kids get any of this?

'The essence goes beyond the thing itself.'
'Be brave. Don't stick to what you see.'
I saw the ivy growing half way across the basement window
but I made a woman's body out of clay.
At first it looked like a woman, then I twisted it.

My father came to pick me up
and got side-tracked by my teacher's mother
who lured him to the huge hodgepodge living room upstairs.
Giant thingless canvases were slung on every wall.
I was polite and waited. He smoked, talked fast, let his eyes wander.

The Long Island School

for Lilian Ruben

Saturday morning – time for art.
I was ten with a plaited head
and matching plaid ribbons tied in neat bows
over rubber bands around the ends of each braid.
The braids were real. So were the rubber bands and ribbons.

Ribbons laced my mind with bars of patterned colours.
Each pair went perfectly with each of my dresses,
my jacket, my Saturday jeans, even my riding jodhpurs.
The ribbons were taffeta, perky,
able to hold out their own rounded loops.

My allowance went by the yard at Woolworth's
on ribbons unwound from cardboard spools,
stretched against a brass ruler embedded in the counter,
then snipped with scissors hanging from the salesgirl's neck.
A snake of white lining paper fell to the floor.

The ribbons were wrapped from pinkie to thumb,
(rhythmically crossing a figure of eight) then eased
off the salesgirl's hand and placed in small paper bag.
Each night, I put the day's ribbons into the laundry.
Later they'd appear in my underwear drawer, folded in pairs.

My father came to pick me up
and got side-tracked by my art teacher's mother.
I saw the ivy growing half way across the basement window.
Then, in the darkened glass, I saw my face, my braids,
my perfect bows. I was polite and waited.

Copley Pond

You don't know the streets of my town
and even if you unfold the map fully,
it's impossible to know where the hills are.
Northern Boulevard, heading east toward Strathmore,
climbs steadily up from Munsey Park,
then down again toward Searingtown Road.
The churches are built on the crest of the hill,
one rising on each corner above Copley Pond.
His was the Lutheran, hers, Congregational.
Beyond the playing field at school,
(west from Munsey Park and then north into Plandome)
his was the oak and hers, the sugar maple.
In the sky, he adopted Orion's belt,
she took to her heart the Milky Way.
He had Bill Haley, she had Nat King Cole.

These divisions worked well.
Neither felt short changed.

On Sunday nights, pale pink in summer,
almost black in winter,
he and she held the crest of the hill between them,
their steeples pegging the sky in place
as Sundays floated past like giant green balloons.
(The churches are marked with crosses on the map.)
One Sunday night in fierce winds of early spring
they began to walk toward one another.
They were wearing their Sunday clothes
and their Sunday shoes.
They had sneaked out of evening worship
without their coats, without a plan.
The hill, held up by the sky, dimpled itself enough
to shelter them into the crest, gust after gust.
They were buttoned, zipped into the day's convention –
a rough tweed jacket and tie for him,
stockings, garter belt, bra and slip for her
under her straight skirt and pale pink twinset.
His fingers stuck to his dampened palms
and the wind parted his Genteel-hardened quiff.
Her tender nipples ached
and rushes of blood fired her body to glowing.

These divisions worked well.
Both were drenched in their own responses.

She wished she'd been able to comb her hair
before his hand moved toward her head,
cupping the base of her neck.
Then he forked his fingers through her hair,
and next, taking the loosened weight of her head,
he tipped it back to let her face face his,
his swanning forward from an awkward height,
his breath caught in his chest, his arteries
beginning to pound, pounding as he teased a space
between her teeth, teeth opening with his tongue
and then, losing the shape of their embrace, they both let go.
His was the holding, the height, the invitation.
Hers was the walk against the wind, the giving in.

These divisions worked well.
They were long, long changed, both together and apart.

They lived in Flower Hill, not far from Copley Pond
(you'll see it marked on the map just below the crosses)
and they walked their dogs, hers brown, his grey,
toward Dogwood Lane and looked surprised when they met.
His family's house had a very steep drive.
Hers had a formal garden at the side.
Sometimes, at night in winter, wanting her,
standing in her backyard, backlit by the moon,
he threw pebbles up to her bedroom window.
She, waking, disbelieving her own eyes,
came down in her nightgown,
opened the door on the south side of the house.
When The Ringling Brothers' Barnum and Bailey Circus,
(the Greatest Show on Earth) came to Madison Square Garden,
(thirty-nine miles west along Northern Boulevard
into the heart of New York City)
she hoped he would borrow his father's car.

'O, take me to the circus in a new pink Pontiac!'
she said, secretly to herself. And he did.

Catching for America

remembering Muriel Rukeyser

She wanted to catch for her country –
(in a century of two world wars) fly balls,
grounders, pop-ups behind the dugout,
finishing off the batters, one by one.
She knew what catchers were supposed to do.
If she had to, she'd hurl the ball like a stone
(one ticked backwards, but not gone foul)
straight down the first base line,
faster than anyone could run
and that would be the end of it.
Like Roy Campanella, behind his mesh mask,
padded with leather, she would squat down,
the stiffened canvas armour across her chest,
an extra wedge in front of her crotch.
She would catch those mighty throws
of Johnny Podres, Don Newcombe, Carl Erskine.
Of course, she wouldn't go out there
(on to Ebbets Field or any other stadium)
in front of all America, unprotected –
her nose and chin exposed,
her cheek bones available for smashing.
No. She would have a purpose-built glove
as well, like a warrior's shield – round, thick,
the fingers not separated from each other.
Finally, unrecognisable, so padded and masked
she is able to squat unafraid behind the plate
and let the balls and strikes pound into her glove.
She will be ready to catch for America.
Most mornings, though more or less insane,
she will walk out on the diamond,
glittering away her impunity like a roman candle
before the Star Spangled Banner, and play ball.

The Geography of Goodbyes

In the hallway of the house
we began to say goodbye.
Everyone gave him some kind of embrace.
A few of us patted his back
in a soothing way, like relatives.
And some clasped him, brooch-like.
Kisses were random, not from everyone.
One woman aimed for his mouth
(I did that too and found his lips
willing and a little apart)
but I noticed he turned and she missed.
Others leaned toward his cheeks.
Then we all moved to the porch
for the 'we must do this more often' part.
And after that, we went down the steps
to the car in front of the house.
He packed his things carefully
as all of us watched from the sidewalk,
helping just enough not to seem idle
but not so much as to make him think
we doubted he could do it alone.
And then, just as we thought he would get
into the car, he said, 'I forgot my guitar.'
All of us followed him back up the steps,
into the house, through the screen door
and back out again on to the porch.
But we didn't go down the steps again.
He cradled the guitar like a child,
holding it close as he went down the steps
then stretching it out away from himself
across the driver's seat as he put it down.
From the porch we heard the car start.
That's where we were when he left.
Standing on the porch. All of us.
We didn't go down the steps again.
We opened the screen door and went in.

Launching from Brooklyn

late summer 2001

for Tom

The ragged end of summer pushes itself out
and the gaudy double hibiscus scrapes the car
as we back down the narrow driveway,
a two-man kayak strapped to the roof.
The boat rams my thigh, swinging as we lower it.
The children shouldn't be swimming here
beside the derelict warehouse, but they are.
I am wearing all the things you gave me to put on.
Yesterday you said her name out loud.
I can see her from here, the anchor to my old hometown,
the blazing torch in my dreams of New York.
Liberty. We're coming to you
in this sliver of orange fibre glass.
Ferries, tugs and ships churn the waves into wakes.
Currents hatchet the basin. The East River,
powerful at its spewing mouth, swills round the Hudson,
ready to spit out the toothpick which seems to be us.
From water level, we look the full length of Manhattan
as if she were Marilyn Monroe with her white skirt
blown up around her waist. We see all there is to see.
The skyline. We name the buildings standing.

Night Light

Picture this.
The corridor between the two rooms is lit.
The light comes from downstairs and fans out
beyond the balustrade, on to the wall.
His house.
He knows the shapes of light and night
and how they interact in his own staircase.
She is the guest.

Should she leave the hall light on downstairs?
Perhaps there is one upstairs which
should be left on instead.
He has gone to bed first,
Leaving her to make these decisions.
When he thinks she is asleep
he comes back to the hall.
There is no light coming
from the gap at the bottom of her door.
He doesn't knock.
He goes straight in, but quietly.
She turns over and faces him.
He thinks he sees her eyes open
but she turns away again
without any other noticeable change.
Imagine this.
Change. As she turns toward him,
she lifts the covers, an invitation, to be sure.
Yes lets his whole body slip in beside her.
Within the picture
of his presence in her room,
he uses his imagination
and sees everything in a different light.
Forget this.
Only take as much as you can handle.
Her body is naked in the light from the hall.
When?
Weeks earlier and every night since then
when she slips off her clothes
wondering about the light, the night, the host.

The Last Sane Thing

I remember the last sane thing you said to me,
though there may have been later things
I judged wrongly and didn't bother to heed –
(like the last sane thing you said to me
which was good advice, but I swept it up
and tossed it into the bin without a thought.)
The second to last thing you said to me
was that the dead were coming for tea.
They would arrive at four
and I should put the kettle on. I did.
I put the kettle on regardless, wondering
who the dead would be when they got here.
The water has boiled, the tea is in the pot
and I lean toward the dead with a tray.
I have found some biscuits to offer them.
(I think you had tea with at least one of them –
if not yesterday, the day before
and possibly we'll have their company tomorrow.)
What was the last sane thing you said to me?
Avoid the dead, you said,
before this new routine
gets rutted into place.

Flights from China

Flights from China could be as late as any flight
I can imagine from anywhere in the world
and China is as far away as you could have gone.

I won't leave till you walk through the door.
I know everything about this house, the heating,
kitchen drawers, curtains that I made myself.

Your mother doesn't picture us changing
places at her bedside since she says
she feels us both beside her all the time.

You and I, living separate lives for twenty years,
can blame our children for keeping stronger continuity
than we ourselves ever managed to undo.

Your plane lands at Heathrow. You take a trolley,
collect your luggage and board the airport shuttle
to the depot where the inter-city buses run.

I follow you in my mind like a wife
as I wait here in Cambridge with your mother.
It feels as if a husband will arrive.

Death in the Family

We are all quiet again.
Until yesterday, the
I phone, you phone, he and she phone
part of our lives was almost all of our lives.
We told one another all the same things
in slightly different words.
We confirmed, affirmed,
reaffirmed and then declared
I did, you did, he and she did.

We had our roles to play
and we played our roles
to the death – the mother, father,
sister, brother, baby roles
which took our breath away.
I love our family more today than ever
I imagined, you imagined,
he and she imagined.
Hush, now. This is our family.

Flower Market with My Son

I see you – just past dawn,
arm bowing above car roofs,
fingers stirring
the early morning,
waving in my direction.
Your grin gears up to call
from behind a truck.
I don't see you.

I see you – this early day,
beyond the tailgate –
you're moving crates
with an instep shove.
Closer to me, your hat
glides to the ground.
You bend behind a bonnet.
I don't see you.

I see you – the day before your wedding,
saunter through boxes
of daffodils unopened –
dry in bunches of ten.
You open past anemones, tulips,
tightly packed rosebuds,
fit for tomorrow's buttonholes.
I don't see you.

3lb 6oz

Born so early,
he managed to reverse all time
until purity didn't need to be a word.
What would it describe?
Attempts to label seemed absurd.

The yin and yang of day and night
hadn't happened yet.
Before impurity had surfaced,
I looked at him, he blinked –
this tiny precursor of stasis.

Extended Family

My daughter wonders who you are,
sitting in the small rocking chair
reading me Rilke and Goethe
you've translated especially for me.

What's available on my shelves
is not exactly right, you say.
Now you and I have the evening
to rock and swivel among the words
you have chosen for me in English.
The poetry leans back and forth,
it dips round and round, unloosened
well beyond the confines of birthright.

My many sons and daughters
push the edges out of what I know
so, so far that I'm giddy with voices
and all their laughing tongues.

Against a Backdrop of Fireworks

There is so little left of the autumn sun
even the garden has gone
underground with its strength.
If the bulbs are swelling
you can't see what they're doing.

The clocks have changed;
even if you think there might be
time to walk home in the twilight,
you are wrong. Right now
it's already dark in front of your house.

Sticks and bottles, you said later,
were smashed on your head, your back.
It was actually lucky, you explained,
lucky you hadn't passed out,
lucky they hadn't broken your legs.

Home was the place you needed to be.
Inside, away from the fireworks,
off the street, sitting in a well-lit room.
Tea. The list of what you wanted
so simple and so short.

Tuning Your Cello

The sounds have been in my head since childhood
so, don't worry, it's not a hardship
for me to draw the bow across the strings
and listen.

Harmony and discord are nearly the same
and you wonder what I will change.
Suddenly I grab one of the ebony pegs
like the ear of a naughty boy.

'Can't you hold on to anything?' I scold.
But the string has no idea
where it has strayed, what has been lost.

The Things You Bring

I don't ask for the things you bring –
not ever being able to think of them.

Like the hot cup of Red Zinger tea this morning
in a thick white outdoor mug
as I sat beside the house-high wall of Virginia creeper.

Every few minutes a scarlet leaf
darted on to my books
and still, I never thought of the tea, Red Zinger.

When you bring me these perfect things
I don't speak.

I take the cup in both my hands.
I know there's nothing you want.

Telling You

I thought of telling you tonight
because I thought you were going
to ask. Yes, I would have said.
It happened once,
and I would have told you
when and where and how
you stood beyond my doorway,
in the hall, one hip jutting out,
your head tilted to one side
as you waited for me
to look up from the papers on my desk.
'Would you like me to help you?'
you said as if it might be
just a cup of tea past midnight –
or a full-scale miracle rescue.

In the doorway late that night,
I imagined you stepping in close
and wrapping a strong rough hand
around to the back of my neck
and letting my head tilt up
as you leaned your own face closer,
and I imagined more than that.
I didn't stop imagining because
I couldn't think of a reason to stop.
It was so late and I was desperate
to be absolved of paperwork
and you stood outside my door
with light from the hall behind you,
one hand in your pocket
and I trembled to think of the other.

What made me think tonight
might be the night for telling you?
It was your thirst. I saw your hand
around a glass of water.

Death Notice

Even though nothing of yours remains in this house,
you show up stunned at the back door,
an arrow sticking out of your chest
and real blood responding,
I didn't see the arrow at first
since you're always slow with me, shy
with me, not really showing me the full
extent of this or any other wound.
Your talk skims to crows and guns,
the outer symbols of losing love to death.
He did it himself with a shotgun, you say.
I see your ribs ridged by the past.
Breathing isn't easy.

We're standing in the kitchen,
back from the table.
You lean against the dresser.
I'm propped against the stove –
as far apart as we can get
and I wonder why we still stand off.
Do you think I will pull the arrow out
and let you bleed to death in front of me?
No. If I could, I'd find a way to comfort you.
I slide out a chair and sit to be closer.
But not too close, not too close now.
Shot guns and screeching crows
are circling in your head above the fallen man.
I know you see straight through the hole in his chest.

With nowhere else to go,
we fall back to a familiar time
when you filled the house with roasted garlic rising
and the table held us all.

Do You Think the Snow Will Stick?

You had taken off your shoes
but not your coat
to stand in my kitchen
before I came in.

It's a treat to see you here
and feel your hands
sizing up the knots now settled
into my shoulder blades.

Has it been that long?
No time at all and you flatter me –
more beautiful than ever.
I read a student's poem – 'Pornography'.

This young poet says he wants
to be touched till morning.
I don't read his next poem
out loud which I regret.

Students these days know so much.
Just a piece of homework face down
on the kitchen table. You kiss me.
Cheek, mouth, cheek, mouth.

Frames of Mind

1 A Short History of Restraint

Scene One takes place in a weaving shed
in a narrow valley of West Yorkshire.

Canvas is a sturdy cloth.
Warp and the weft are exactly the same
and the weave comes together in equal parts.
No dye need ever be used.
Reels of yarn, lightly flecked,
loaded beside the deafening looms,
let long fibres cling to each other
in a tight, simple cross hatch.
They have not been bleached.
Nothing has been taken away.
One future for canvas is hammocks –
lengths as long as the distance between two trees,
perhaps striped, first with natural threads,
then green, then natural again, then red.
Or deckchairs, awnings, mailbags, straps.

Scene Two takes place in an upstairs factory
in one of the alleys, back of Piccadilly.

Bodice Front: cut on the fold.
Bodice Back: cut two.
Top Sleeve: cut two.
Under Sleeve: cut two.
Binding at the neck: cut double.
Cuffs? No Cuffs. There will be no cuffs.
The sleeves will be cut long enough to cover
the hands. Very strong seams will be stitched
across the end of the finger tips.
Tapes will be inserted,
long enough to wrap a man across his chest –
and to wrap a man across his chest again.
Unless you are making gloves,
the word *hand* will never be written
on any of the brown paper pattern pieces

hanging against the sweatshop wall.
Even *arms* will not be written.
All the words written are for the layers
outside the skin, beyond the man –
they are not to do with his body
but to do with what covers it,
or rocks it in the afternoon sun
held by a length of canvas
slung between two trees
halfway up a mountain, his red-blond head
propped up on a small blue pillow,
packed hard, filled with kapok.
The only words ever used describe
the shapes which hold a man in place –
the yoke across his shoulders,
the stitches at the ends of his mitted sleeves
seamed beyond his fingertips
securing the tapes which extend
beyond the breadth of his open arms.

Scene Three takes place in an upstairs room
of a large terraced house in South Manchester.

His arms are not in the sleeves.
His hands are not in the mitts.
He holds up the jacket in front of himself
like an outfit to choose for a paper doll.
In one hand he has a tool which does the opposite of sew –
a tiny steel hook with a sharp blade tucked inside its curve.
The canvas seams are perfect,
making hard, clear mounds on either side
of the linen threads which bridge
the pieces made for him
that the pattern-cutters named.
This tool – Oh, this tool!
He takes it in his hand
and brings it closer to his chest,
folding back his seams
with the lowering of his own eyelids,
finding exactly the place
to let the metal touch the thread.
If he cuts one, the next one will loosen.

2 Dead Lock

It's lock out and lock in
with no key hidden in the usual place,
no easy access, no surprises guaranteed.
This yellow room keeps me intact
against an onslaught of poking fingers
but I'm yolk soft inside my trumped up shell.
A child in a trunk, a baby in a basket
staking life on a large Victorian key.
You've been talking to dead men
and their voices have talked to you.

It's lock out and lock in
with me hiding in an upstairs room
and you ringing, calling, pounding.
My barricade works against your fist
your mouth, your eyes, your heaving chest
but your voice carries and the dead men
downstairs set their feet inside the corridor
and start to scurry toward the stairs.
You've been plotting with dead men
and their plots have entered your head.

This lock out and lock in
seems no more real than a child's game.
It's the mouse and the hickory clock,
the flame and nimble Jack,
the blind mice feeling their way along the walls.
As soon as either of us thinks of the stairs,
we create the shape of a house
and all the rooms open into the well.
You've been drawn by dead men
and it's clear, they're drawn by you.

3   Havoc

Just look at the dented lawn –
coconuts, avocados, bowling balls
from nowhere. How could you?
Limbs snapped off the pear tree
just because you decide
to chin-up your entire bulk.
And the litter is so careless –
a silver bracelet tossed
behind the bare magnolia,
a dagger from daddy, poked
into a birch as if you and he
had a smutty secret going.
Fruit, oozing, stuck with pins,
candles, sandalwood reduced
to wicks in sloppy pools.
Eggs from the china chicken
roll in your palm before you
smash them into the sink.
No lighter and no matches.
You resort to a gas flame
and singe your orange hair.
I smell the burning
and the shattered promise
of scented wax.
You've crossed the line
and I am roped to you.
Then you say out loud
'There isn't enough room here.'
And I say, 'Go on, go further.'

4   The Weeping House

You come and go in this house like wind which stirs
the sky and then drops over-ripe meteors of gloom.
Just look at the pitted lawn you've left behind.
The window shades flap, judder and gape
like giant blinking eyelids to the street.
The doors are wide open, fanning, creaking,
chanting their taunting little songs to their architraves.
'Keeps is for keepers. You're surely lost,' they say.

I've let you go, wishing the garden were bigger
than you need, wanting the night to be darker
than the midnight blue already blotting your sight.
There will never be enough colour in the dark
to paint a true likeness of even one of your demons,
yet you rush toward all of them at once,
your pallet dripping across the doorjambs,
trailing gaudy traces of your unrest. In and out,
you go as far as you can and then you go further.
You track new mud upstairs, then down again.

I feel the chill of autumn gusts forced beneath
the upstairs doors. You slam your way out below.
Loss is for losers. All week you've kept a rifle
under your bed, pumped and trained on mirrors.
Finders find everything – stray bullets, shooting stars.
I see you. I've had to stand on tiptoe and hide behind
the faded blue of scattered cotton flowers. Out there,
rotting leaves barely keep the underworld down.
The house can't take this traffic any more.
Exhausted, it closes its black and blue thighs against
the draft, curls in to brace against the garden wall.

5   Two a Day

Two new tragedies a day and that's all!
They'll be limited and strictly regulated –
one in the morning and one in the afternoon.
It's important to keep the numbers down
and protect you from the liberty of excess.

Take today, for example. Not batting an eye,
you racked up four new tragedies, a virtual A&E –
two in the morning and two in the afternoon.
Count them: one death, two heart attacks and a rape,
not to mention the dead man's post mortem coronary.

Yesterday, you scared me with cancer talk.
Sarcomas, lymphomas, melanomas and leukaemia –
four in the morning and four in the afternoon.
Colorectal, cervical, testicular and prostate,
giving a full case history for each one.

Last week, you created an AIDS epidemic,
bigger than anyone could have imagined –
Africa in the morning and China in the afternoon.
Someone else did the paperwork, of course
but you had to travel and give first-hand accounts.

No wonder I've decided to take you in hand
looking for lesser tragedies to impact on our lives –
one in the morning and one in the afternoon
is quite enough, even if the level is drastically cut
to a rain-drowned worm and a broken fingernail.

6 Water's Way

Beside the bath, enveloped by the steam,
afraid to let his body be submerged,
he stands. The water's way is too extreme.

His dread of drowning haunts him like a dream
of naked Romans trying to muster courage
to take the plunge, enveloped by the steam.

'Slip in! It won't take long before you're clean.'
The sudsy water calls – enticing, urgent.
He stares (the water's way is too extreme)

then whips the bubbles, frothing them to cream.
He sees his hand, stripped white as bone, emerge
beside the bath, enveloped by the steam.

'My hand, my hand!' An agonising scream,
a drenching cry, dissolving to a dirge,
he chants, 'The water's way is too extreme.'

To cleanse, to purify, what does it mean?
Lose everything? Be skinless, sinless, purged?
Now in the bath, enveloped by the steam,
he's sure the water's way is too extreme.

7 Disarmed

He dropped it. He made no attempt to hide.
If he could swallow his own sword, I thought
the trick would be, head back and open wide.

The heavy club he held down at his side
was menacing enough, his muscles taut.
He dropped it. He made no attempt to hide.

Shouting was the next offence he tried.
Grunts and bellows, belly groans were wrought
by demons' tricks his head had opened wide.

They moved in close so fast, attacked his pride,
exposed the slingshot tucked inside his coat.
He dropped it. He made no attempt to hide.

Unarmed, unwashed, unable to abide
the ragged phantom warriors he'd fought.
Retreat, retreat. Head back and open wide.

For days and nights all weapons were denied
until he snatched the dagger I had brought.
Then dropped it. He made no attempt to hide.
Surrendering, head back all opened wide.

8 Cheetham Hill to Crumpsall

on a pass from Manchester General Hospital

You say it's like Brooklyn here –
windswept with litter – attitude in the air.
Who couldn't notice this jagged cityscape,
scattering people from everywhere
who cover their heads,
in so many different ways?

Like a prison break, we're out
and no one knows how free,
moseying up the main drag,
iron-shuttered, tinged
with all the hues and tongues of Manchester.
It's another melting pot, not rich enough
to keep the riff-raff out.

This is why we feel at home
eating our Caribbean dumplings
from a brown paper bag, hopping across
puddles that ooze through broken slabs.
We lick our fingers as if the Atlantic
had splashed us with a sugar wave.

We've cigarettes in our pockets
(someone gave me a lighter this week!)
and a bottle of Dr Pepper waits in the car –
our too-new, too-silver car
parked in the alley. It gives us away.
You and I, so comfortably (we start to laugh)
out of place, just like everyone else.

9 Home Life

We talk about you
at breakfast after the boiling water
has been poured into the cafetière
and before we push the plunger down.

We talk about you
at lunchtime even though
it's just a sandwich in the car.
We find spaces between mouthfuls.

We talk about you
while drinking cups of tea,
deciding who will do your washing
and who will buy the olives.

We talk about you
when we get home.
Lukas says it took you half an hour
to fold a shirt today.

We talk about you
instead of the news.
You are our news, unrest,
connection to the world.

We talk about you
while one of us cooks
and the other slumps at the table
wishing it was her turn to cook.

We talk about you
as we catch spaghetti threads
on forks and twirl them round
as if this really made a difference.

We talk about you
to someone on the phone
while the TV is on. At last,
we turn everything off.

Keeping the Boys Home

They muttered out loud for you to hear –
Pretty boy, gay boy, nancy boy, queer,
voices low, their skateboards tucked
under their arms, clumsy and squint
the wheels, well greased, whirring, purring.
Too dangerous out there. Come back quick.
You're too pretty and they're too thick.

They shouted across the street from the bank,
Hey, Paki, you Muslim shite! Terrorist wank,
even though traffic whizzed back and forth
and you kept on walking the other way
they couldn't be bothered, strutting, crossing.
Too dangerous, dressed so smart and slick,
you're too Asian and they're just sick.

They picked up stones and dared you to run
Hey giant! Fee, fi, fucker and fum!
Just angry twits with rocks and cans
pelting your back, but missing your head,
knee high only, yapping, scrapping.
Lilliputians waving sticks,
you tower over these puny pricks.

Keeping you in is my last resort,
making our home secure as a fort.
'We can take it,' you're quick to assure me,
giving as good as you're getting. Letting
the pressure defuse, turning your cheek.
You think hate knocks? It's tied to a brick.

Paces

You went through your paces for me,
sticking, blocking, kicking
extending your left leg back
for a perfect forward stance –
a warrior, flying glorious flags
above each new technique.
Oh yes, I was dazzled by your fists
and by your faultless footwork.

You went through your rhythms for me,
hands slapping, fingers tapping,
palms like giant lion paws, pounding
on drum heads with the fury
of a flying heart believing
it can beat the air like wings.
From what I hear, from what I see,
the sky is not about to drop you.

You went through all of this for me
before you spoke. Pointed words
at first were arrows into armour.
Then softer words, my name and then
no words at all. I've dropped my guard
and you are standing here as if
you'd never moved before.
Outpaced, both of us, caught still.

Cellar Dance

'A man dancing naked in the cellar'
is not a story to dine out on.
It is just one of the secrets of the house
kept in the dark, next to the laundry room,
though lots of people saw him.

I mean he had music, for Christ's sake
and rows of benches for the audience.
It was no accident, no chance event,
not something I stumbled on in the dark
without being led to the witness seat
by a young man with a torch
who invited me to sit down, and I did.

I could have teased you, made a story
of the gradual unfolding – for instance,
how I first saw his shoulder
with the tiniest bit of light behind it
and I could see he was not wearing a shirt.
He was sitting behind a big box
which let only his upper torso show.
I didn't give the rest of his body a thought.

Not until he stood up, holding a tiny red light
in each of his hands.
No. Light is too strong a word –
just parts of the dark
which were no longer black,
but had turned red instead.

He danced with his arms in the air
like a brand new bear in the forest,
as if he knew no other creatures were looking.

Of course I looked. Everyone did –
quite hard too, forcing our eyes around the dim
edge of his body against the flaking cellar walls
to see what parts of him flounced to the music
describing a man, only a man
dancing naked in the cellar.

Sharing

If I have to share a bathroom with you much longer
one of us might leave a hair of some kind or other
in the tub, or an implement for beauty – razor, tweezers,
loofah, pumice, hairbrush, back brush – showing itself
brazenly on a shelf or leaning like a tart against a tap.
So far, we have managed to keep our private potions –
our jars, tubes and bottles of preparations to ourselves,
carrying them back and forth from our rooms to the bathroom
in large plastic bags, but I refuse to play the charade any longer.
I mean, I could – I could do it by repeating the past –
by putting on my glasses whenever I scrub down the tub
to be perfectly sure no wisp of anything hinting at human,
formerly part of my body, had strayed on to any porcelain surface,
mirror or floor tile, and that all of my bottles and jars and bars
were packed away at the end of every one of my ablutions.
You see, I don't want to know that kind of stuff about you
and for every day I face this risk, the margin for error expands
around the edges due to long-term familiarity of our routine
which has made me less inclined to vigilance and falsely secure.
If I have to share a bathroom with you much longer,
any day now I will walk naked from my room into the hallway
unwashed, ungroomed and shedding. Beautiful.

Premature

for Frankie Armstrong

White hair, white stick
and a laugh like lilies of the valley,
following her from room to room –
tinkling bells, as she faced the sunniest
window and declared it a perfect place.

'There is very little I actually see,'
she said, letting her voice rise to the rafters,
then fall fast to prod the maple floor.
She tested for echoes, fullness, space,
the way a painter considers light.

She knew about light already –
white hair, white stick
and the scent of the garden,
premature as a rampant spring
bucking the frost, regardless.

Nice

Being nice to you, I did not complain
when you forgot to lock the back door
or, when I let you use my desk, you didn't put
my stacks of papers back where they had been.
I let you be right about Whitworth Street
and I didn't mind that you left selected items
of washing-up which you yourself had not used.

The only trouble with being nice to you
is that I am preoccupied with creating lists
of all the ways I am being nice to you
in spite of your irritating, blinkered behaviour.
I, on the other hand, am attaining sainthood,
at least during the short period which remains
before I re-enter the house with a gun.

All Day Goodbyes

1   Morning Goodbye

You came across the lawn
to say goodbye,
sliding your foot on the yoga mat.
The skid unbalanced you
as you teetered the four steps
to the bottom of the stairs
leading from the garden to the porch.
The first step up steadied you.

On the second step you were high enough
to reach my lips for the first time.
Dead on the lips, quickly,
then two steps back down.

2   Afternoon Goodbye

Just the usual.
You are always looking for a way
to let me be taller
than I really am.

Whenever we are on the stairs
and I'm ahead of you,
I turn around.
Sometimes, it's hello,
sometimes goodbye
as our hands slip easily
around the backs of our T-shirts
and our heads nuzzle down.

Today it is goodbye.
I keep goodbyes on a separate shelf
from the loosely packed hellos
which I store with the cornflakes and popcorn.

Goodbyes, these sardine soldiers
wriggling their fins free to salute
come up behind me in quick shoals
all a-flutter, shimmering,
like tears in oil,
sweeping me up in their frenzy
of bye bye bye,
bye bye bye.

3   Evening Goodbye

I was already outside the house,
car keys in my hand,
bag on my shoulder,
when I saw you behind the blinds.

I blew you a kiss right through the glass,
then hurled it between the painted slats,
across your desk
to your cheek.

You got it, all right.
Your cheek flinched with the impact,
lifting the corners of your mouth.
Goodbye, I mouthed back from outside.

Confidence

More important than what he said
was that no one else should know.
Do you promise, he kept asking.
And it was easier to say yes over and over
in order not to stop the flow.
It's strange, he said. I can't explain it.
The feeling is very strong
and it moves through me like water.
Are you sure, he said, that you won't tell
Anyone – not even that I spoke to you?
I continued to agree and he went on,
I can't describe what happens
or why it happens or why I even
feel the need to tell you or find out
what it could possibly mean.
The feeling, I said. What is it like?
Well, he said (and by now I was
getting a little impatient with his
reluctance to put it into words),
it's something I've never felt before.
Is it in your body, I asked
and that seemed to make it easier for him
and he said, yes. Fear is in my body.
In every part of it, racing around.
And I said, excellent. Fear is good.
And feeling fear is especially good
and telling the fear and moving on
and knowing what is there, under your skin
whether you like it or not,
scared to death, is absolutely fine.
Did he think I would just turn around
and tell everyone I know
about his fear and diminish him
as a man in their eyes?
Doesn't he know a giant is being made?

Scene Shift

Here, we've been sitting around the kitchen
trying to remember movie stuff –
like who made *Nil by Mouth*,
and did Brando say
'What have you got?' in *The Wild Ones*
or maybe it was James Dean.
We managed breakfast anyway.
Some fruit, toast, no jam – nothing cooked,
and not much remembered at all
by the time you phoned.

You can see fjords from her garden, you say,
and people speak English whenever you approach.
Earlier, there were sword forms on the lawn
because her Tai Chi teachers had, indeed, come.
Her parents watched as the gift of their skill
was given to their daughter's practice place.
You'd sat with her open coffin in the house
as the sun spilled in. A perfect day, you tell me.
Crystal clear. They've just taken her away
and the rest of you will follow in cars at eleven.

I tell you I love you.
I love you for taking your sword to Norway.
I love you for being her teacher
and for knowing what part you play.
I love you for being a man – clear, sun flooded.

One of Them

You have become one of them
wedged into the corner of the striped sofa,
reaching your right arm high
behind you to find your friend's hand.

You find it and he is amazed
that it is nearly right side up –
that is, thumb up
to meet his hand in a clasp.

The two of you shake –
comrades, one of each other's,
saying good night – how good
it was to meet again.

When you and I say good night,
there are no contortions to go through –
just a slip-hug, a lip-brush
a night-latch, a click-shut.

Judo Mad

She was afraid judo would make her stupid
but her trainer said it was the best thing there is.
Head injuries aren't everything, he said.

Her father didn't even know where she'd been
the day she squeezed in through the front door,
exhausted, her rucksack on her back.

She made him put the newspaper down.
Stand up, she said to him in a grown-up voice,
before she dropped him to the floor.

Fathers are like lightning rods.
They just take what daughters give them
right into the ground and then over they go,

a tumbling stack of daddiness,
weakened by a flaw at the root. Certainly,
she felt insane that day, but not stupid.

'It's Only Time'

Stephen Merritt's song plays in the background

Her arms above her head, turning in the kitchen like a Sufi
she hears the words 'it's only time' and circles the table faster.

The kitchen door is open and the passing frames hold
armloads of sky, trees, then cups, saucers and plates.

The garden has finished with spring. It's done with colour
except for green and an overgrowth of geraniums.

'I will be free' she hears as she tumbles toward the living room,
a tiny tornado on tiptoe, drawn to the field of the music.

In the cellar, the big white appliances rotate, then spin,
turning over her clothes, pulling her sleeves inside out.

Finally the layers of the house relax into their footings
and she patrols the halls, then makes a final safety check.

On the brink of dizziness, what is it she sees out there?
A sky hung with ripcords begging to be tugged.

Does this mean that heaven will keep opening up forever
as she twirls toward the door, spun out to a ceilingless lawn?

Her arms above her head, turning on the grass like a Sufi
she hears 'it's only time' and she knows it's only time.

The Young Taoist Transcends His Body

In less than two hours,
he managed to move his whole body
through his hands,
as the centres of his palms opened.
His eyes widened,
the pupils spread out into blue irises
and his mind released
like the top of a baby's head.
The walls, covered in murals,
turned to paper as the night sky
slid in through the cracks
and his own thoughts slipped out,
shaped like Chinese kites,
self igniting, tails on fire, soaring
in competition with the moon.

Let me tell you, the moon
was not a sliver that night.
It was one day off being full
and he chased it shamelessly.
A paper dragon, flames lashing
his own body from behind,
he raged, red-orange across the sky
with ground glass glued
to his reeled out string.
He could have cut the moon to shreds
since all the sky belonged to him
and all the fire was his plaything.
What a furious rush of wind he made,
what a stirring. I tell you,
it was a glorious way to go out.

Passing

We passed, going opposite ways –
our two cars moving so slowly
that he was able to gesture to me
by tapping his front tooth
with his index finger as if to say
'You have a bit of spinach, just there,'
and I let my tongue swoop around
my mouth until I found it. Carefully
I picked it off with my thumbnail
and then nodded a little thank you
which I fear he might have misread
as the bodies of our vehicles slipped
past one another, narrowly missing
cars, the wall, side-view mirrors jutting.

White China Bowl

for Rose

This morning you handed me a white china bowl –
a deeper one than I would have chosen myself.
It is not that the bowls were out of reach
or that I would not have been able to choose.

Nothing stood between me and the bowls
until you did. You reached toward them
and I sat down, waiting like a child at my place,
fingering the box of cereal, lifting it, shaking it.

Then I took the bowl from your hands
and placed it on the table in front of me.
You went to the fridge to get the milk.
I lifted the spoon.

Consultant

on the Neuro-Psychiatric Ward

He thinks they shouldn't operate
but doesn't say it in so many words
to her nor them. Not yet.

She's young and doesn't speak English.
There isn't much to go on. They know
she's very mixed up in her mind.

One of those maybe-yes, maybe-no cases
consultants are called in to assess.
He doesn't give them a bill for his advice

(which he doesn't give them either).
He sits at her bedside
straight through all his billable hours,

marvelling at her, sensing her
speak the language she knows
inside her mind.

The Widow Puts Off Grief

'Fifty dead husbands.'
She winced at the words
but let the comment pass
knowing he meant well
and wanted to help.
(Absurd, she thought.
Can't he count?
A lot of them are still alive.)
'Just how live are they?'
he asked, as if he thought
collectively they might be
on their one last leg.
She reminded him
not to villainise her
just because the numbers
involved were large.
He then resorted
to a breakfast TV approach,
'Do you think you will marry
often again in the future?'
to which she triumphantly
replied, 'If you say *yes*,
tomorrow will do nicely.'

Limits

Maybe we have gone too far
and whatever else we think of
will push us further and further apart.
I can hardly offer you an orange
without the skin meaning
you are too tough and the colour
saying that subtlety sucks.
If you go out and don't say where
or if the doorbell rings
and the person who has rung it
is a stranger to me who's come
to take you somewhere in a car,
I feel like bursting into tears.
If sex were not unthinkable for us
I would do everything in the book
until you begged for mercy
from the rawest ravishing I would
thrust in your face and elsewhere
until you slapped the mat
to indicate that enough is enough.
As it is, we just don't know.

Soup Course

She had already put the cream into the soup,
so you can see how late in the game it was.
The dinner bell had rung already and everyone
was heading toward the piping hot pot.
Full of steaming soup, she held the ladle
by its rounded bowl, high above her head,
hot as it was, even dripping on her hair.
The handle could have flown a flag,
standing so proud and so straight up.
We thought she was going to speak
because of this triumphant pose.
Feeling the moment, she stage-whispered
'Here's to you!' directly to the soup.

Immaculate Mother

The grown-up children sat at the table
just as they used to do –
expectant, excited, reasonably polite,
seeing their mother partly as food,
partly as hands, partly as a smile.
She was not a virgin but all the same,
they draped her image in a pale blue robe
and tucked her hair under a snug white scarf,
(figuratively speaking, of course).

Having spent the afternoon with her lover
(after she'd chopped the Chinese vegetables
and put the soup stock up to boil, then turned
it off with the lid in place to keep the heat
for a bit more simmering while she was out)
she rushed back after some time, during which
her lover's whiskers had grown a millimetre –
just enough to turn his chin to stubble
scraping her face to a Szechuan glow
she feared might ignite her hair.

Even before the meal began
she complained of the heat in the kitchen,
made excuses for her burning cheeks.
Her grown up children hadn't noticed.
They saw their mother as they'd always seen her,
partly as food, partly as hands, partly as a smile.
She showed a certain spark, but they couldn't place it.

An Amusing Little Breakfast

Are we amused,
my adorable little spoon-fed muse,
or is it getting too charred around the edges for you?

Amusing, still,
it's possible these words are the last I write
which keep you in my mind, heart-tucked, pen poised.

Will you be amused
when no new breakfast is put on a plate,
arranged carefully and handed across the table to you?

I was amused – once,
my dearest little muse-muffin. Remember?
I opened you up with my finger tips, crumb by delectable crumb.

Pre-Op

They had taken her blood in the afternoon –
lots and lots of blood she told me.
They'll be keeping it aside for afterward.
She looked as pale as a china doll.

That's why I did it the first time.
I kissed her cheek, right on Oxford Road
in front of a concrete blocked-off building
which had no door in the front.

A second time, I did it without reason.
She told me dates for admission and surgery.
I know appointments don't call for kisses
and kisses don't turn to blood. I know this.

Verse Vampire

She holds up the singled-out pages
in front of her like trophies.

He sees clearly the remnants
of coagulated glue along their edges.

The numbers are marked in bold ink
which bleeds through to both sides.

These pages, dripping with poems
carry deep impressions of her teeth.

Her bite marks are easy to see –
the sheets were ripped from the spine.

She curls up her mouth and looks at him
while holding a flimsy page of truce.

He sees her rings of hardened blood –
a simile slips from her swollen lips.

The Good Sister and the Good Brother

Don't you remember that Sunday, last summer
on the patio with the cats and the honey lemon water
when you walked on your hands, high stepping
across to the magnolia and then crumpled, giggling?

Remember how your sister started to cry,
her tears streaking, salt sticking to her lashes,
her hands scooping the tears, flinging them off.
She was beside herself, stricken for your sake.

'My darling little brother has fallen here,
upside down, from the pose he'd struck to impress.'
What can the little brother do, save entertain,
save apply himself, save demonstrate allegiance?

And how can the sister soothe, one or two fingers
apart like a comb, pushing his hair up from the roots?
She tells him, everything will be fine —
the summer is perfect for brothers and sisters.

Beach Story

for Nina Cassian

Her blue dress is still running on the beach,
God help it! If only I could scoop it into my arms
without the awful moment of knowing it's empty.

Cotton, sleeveless, it holds the shape of a girl
only by the grace of a meagre breeze
dancing down from the dunes with the sun.

By evening, there's no wind left anywhere
along the shore. The horizon is truly flat
and the tide makes its final choice of change.

Her moon face and her moon head float
skyward into the waiting painted arms
of her one-eyed, beautiful bridegroom.

Children, this is the story of Nina
running on the beach. Nina, running
for life, Nina running for love.

The Giveaway

All day I tried to give things away.
I put sweets on plates and handed them round.
I put shirts on backs and buttoned them up.
I put words on screens and printed them out.

But I didn't have any success.
At the end of the day, nothing was gone
and my arms ached from offering.
Some days don't go as planned. They stay.

Upgraded

You sized me up and up and up
until I was a superstar, magician,
goddess, a bloody A-List oracle.

Out of the blue, I now know things
I had only dreamed of before —
blue things, green things, silver things.

'Think of a colour,' I tease you
as the pale pink dawn cracks open.
Before you think of it, I know.

Mentor

I believe because you believe
is not exactly true, but nearly.

When I see you stand up
my knees and ankles flex.
When you begin to speak
my ears perk up and twitch
in the rhythm of your words,
not wanting to miss one dip,
one pirouette of meaning.
Don't worry. It's not your fault.

A court of law would let you off
without assigning responsibility
even though I look like you,
act like you and say what you say.
I shout your words in the street,
I broadcast them on TV and radio,
I post them on my website
and quote you as my source.

Did you think the future
would happen some *other way*?

My Last Lover

My last lover (as in, *previous*)
    You may be comparing yourself with him
    though you don't even know his name, his drinking habits
    his levels of lust, or his attitude toward underwear.
    None of this stops you thinking he didn't amount to much.

My last lover (as in, *at long last*)
    Now you're talking! Finally after long last, here he is,
    on his knees in the moonlit bedroom, loosening
    a few bits of clothing, taking off his watch and leaving it
    on the bedside table for the foreseeable future.

My last lover (as in *long lasting*)
    Let him last forever, night after night, tirelessly
    taking me this way and that, beyond counting,
    over the top with how long and how long lasting.
    Let there be lashings of lust at last, lasting long.

My last lover, (as in, *final*)
    No one will be comparing him to anything or anyone
    because no one would have known at the time or even later
    if he is or was or would be in the future, my last lover.
    Language of lovers, a letdown, at last, at long last, last.

Still Things Left

'There are still things left to enjoy,'
my therapist commented casually,
for which I will write him a cheque
at the end of the month.

If I pay him a little more, I wonder,
will he tell me what they are?
If I pay him a little less,
will therapy be one of them?

II
Younger Men Have Birthdays Too

Younger Men Have Birthdays Too

Older and older and older...
I love the way you age around me
holding me like a newborn in your arms,
teaching my lips to find you in the dark.

Older and older and older...
you grow around me as all your birthdays
celebrate the end and the beginning
and this flickering tenderness in between.

Love Watch

In the morning
if I wake up early
I can watch you sleeping.
I'm besotted
as a brand new mother
observing the greatest
miracle on earth.

'He breathes in and out'
I might think to myself
and take all the credit
as if I had invented lungs
and what to do with them.
But I have done almost
nothing on your behalf.

You came to me
a man, fully formed.
How your eyelids close
as you fall asleep
I have no idea,
or of the process
which will open them.

I love not knowing
when or how your eyes
will see me again.
Sometimes sleep
seems to keep us apart.
Sometimes I know certainly
I am alone.

Gamble

The stakes are high in this game.
On the days I win
I win more than I know I want.

On other days I lose more
than I'm able to imagine.
I consider folding my hand.

Instead, for no reason, I fan it
and you hit me with a high one
and I just keep on rolling.

Loving Parents

Your daughter is learning to speak.
My son's thoughts have long been strung into words,
wrapped on a reel and let loose,
lacing praise and kind thoughts
through your heart without the slightest pinch.

He loops your daughter in sweet talk.
I do up the Velcro on her shoes
and she runs straight toward you.
As you toss her up against the sky,
I see what my son sees in your face.

Purification

I feed the length of you through me
like a yogi with an endless rope –
ecstatic and clean as a whistle.

Threaded through my bones
you're the wick, sealed in place –
smouldering, dripping wax.

Are we afraid of blasphemy
in this communion with each other –
binding us, unwinding us, igniting?

Secret

Our secret is the best thing that ever happened to us
or to me, I should say, since you told me the secret
and I just listened. But I have equal share in it now.

It is ours, moored inside a soap bubble bottle
above our heads, precariously suspended
by threads too fine to see with the naked eye.

I try not to see anything in it at all, now
when I look up at our quite burdensome
bottle which reminds me not to speak.

I've nearly forgotten how. I never talk about you
or anything we did together or about our friends
for fear our secret will blurt out of their mouths.

Everything is sealed. Building the ship
through the bottle neck was our most exciting time,
imagining the day it would lurch down the slipway.

Restaurant

People are eating and passing food across this table
upon which you have immobilised my right hand
against the wood with your own firm left hand.

Everyone can see you have got me
anchored in place, your hobbled left-handed lover
still able to eat, but not wander off.

There is no struggle whatsoever to be seen.
Not a finger of mine slips through any of yours
as part of a cunning strategy for escape.

Tamed and tethered, I graze contentedly
in front of the very friends who think me wild.
It excites them. In their dreams you pin me down.

Urgency

Quick! My tan is fading
and that's the least of it.
Don't wait another day
if you want to find me
still in one piece, pulse
pumping, heart throbbing
breath panting in and out
enough to put mist on a mirror.

I can see you,
even behind my back
dancing in circles around
me winding yourself in
for the power yet to come,
coiling tighter in loops
just in the nick of time,
to spring. Spring! Let loose!

Cooking for You

Here's me, cooking for you
in green satin underwear –
(of course other garments too, on top.
Trousers, T-shirt, a butcher's apron –
even oven gloves from time to time.)

I am a proper-looking cook.
If you happened into the kitchen,
you would think me as plausible
as anyone else who might
chop, cut, toss, stir.

But the inner layer of green
affects the sauces in subtle ways –
an earthy undercurrent flavours
the outer trappings of every dish,
peeking through the garnishes.

You are probably thinking
mint or some cool consequence
of the colour, relating itself to food.
But the green I'm wearing is more
a traffic-light kind of green.

It tells me 'go' and I do –
I go directly to the chillies,
the cayenne and the paprika.
I am liberal with sprinkling,
my palette poised to slam into red.

Journeys with my Phantom Lover

The places I have taken you
do not bear mentioning.
Another and another
without a passport, visa
or a ticket of your own.

Travelling across borders,
stuffed with documents
for myself, I smuggle you
as if I were a desperate mule,
oblivious to all the risks.

Surely my contraband
will not be found, I tell myself
as I stride across the lines,
pitting you against authority.
Phantom lover, my true transporter.

Flying to Spain

It's possible
you are there, still,
in England, asleep in my bed
guarding our latest secrets
with the arc of your body.
Every breath turns you slowly,
rearranges your legs,
your hips, your back,
as one long arm opens, a wing
falling across my empty pillows.

It's possible
that the secrets are sinking
into the feathers under your arm.
In your sleep I know
that you remember my mouth
as much as you remember your own.
Love and the words of love
and the loving are all there,
swilled together, savoured,
exclaiming our names.

Tuscany

Tuscany tugs
with its terracotta sunburnt grip
to divert my attention as I sweat,
climbing the steep stone paths
through sturdy medieval gates
to a safer place. Protected
above the roofs, I see the pantiles
blanketing the houses below.

I see how these jigsaw blocks
of ridges, rolls and curves
have found their own scheme
of interlocking in full view,
held by the weight of each other,
the sun penetrating their laps.
The sky is doing to terracotta,
in Tuscany, what only blue can do.

The Same as What?

While you were sleeping
I used some parts of your body
to do things to myself.

You didn't wake
and they felt very nice,
but it's not really the same thing.

Red Wings

Your long red-shirted arms flailed
like giant crane wings on the balcony
as if they would lift you, let you glide over
Kentish Town and further north to Hampstead.

I would hitch a ride on your back,
brave as Amelia Earhart with goggles
looking down on London, waiting
until we saw the trees and ponds of the Heath.

Then you could land on a sloping meadow
and wrap me in those long red arms
and we'd roll together down into a thicket,
tumbled, entwined around each other.

It was just a bit of dancing on the balcony
as the sun sank through the pink sky
and you got so carried away. And I?
I went every bit of the distance with you.

My Brave Pink

My brave pink/purple, front-line heart
(a proper little cliff-hanger with wings,
parachute and fitted on–impact airbags)
is on the ground in smithereens.

Too high up for the safety valve to open
and too quick falling to unfold the wings.
Airbags might as well have been rocks,
once the bottom had been hit.

Don't bother to scrape it up
or reshape it into some two-bit valentine.
I don't want lace, ribbons or a message.
Show mercy. Leave it blank.

Ourselves

Promise you won't touch me
or change the course of what I do.
I need your word on this, you see
I could confuse myself with you –

your hand mine, your eyes mine.
Even if you want to lose yourself
in secluded places that I find,
you can't. Detached, I'm by myself,

exposed, yet somehow trusting
that your word will hold you back.
We're cut to the quick, lusting,
both bound by this lonely pact –

I for myself,
you for yourself.

The Radio Next Door Is Far Too Loud

It's quieter than I had expected,
though why I think about levels of noise,
is beyond me. It was never loud.

Even when you sang, it was softly,
under the instrumental music, just enough
to dust the words across our feet, while dancing.

Not really boisterous people, you and I.
Quiet while eating – just a murmur or two
about articles in the *Guardian* or a friend.

We never shouted messages at full voice
from the top of the stairs, reminding each other
about love or to post a letter or get some milk.

But we managed to say these things
nevertheless. We said them while looking
into each other's faces, directly, not flinching.

The quiet part is that there are no words
and there are no faces. No lyrics for tunes,
not even faint feet and no dancing.

You Have a Daughter

She draws you first to a window
and then to the back door of the house,
where you look in, over the garden gate.

She is sitting in her high chair
at breakfast, the spoon tight in her fist
and yoghurt all over her cheeks.

I can see her too, inside the house
full of stairs and blinds which are
still pulled down in the upstairs rooms.

You left me on the street at the front
looking straight through. I see you.
I see you just beyond your daughter.

Carrot Wheels

Poking my fork around in the dregs
of last week's fridge-clearance pasta sauce,
I found the carrots which certainly got there
by way of your hands and the vegetable peeler.

I never peel carrots. What would be the point?
Some scare about insecticides embedding themselves
in the outer skins which could, in excess, kill you
but it might take fifty years. I don't have that long.

They looked like badly chiselled 20p pieces –
not evenly rounded, burnt-orange pound coins,
though there weren't very many of them left –
just enough to remind me of you and the peeler.

The GUM Clinic

1 Sex Talk at the GUM Clinic

Did she say vigorously or rigorously,
to question how we've been doing it?

Was it abrasive or embracive, she asks,
when the parts of us got together?

I told her I couldn't really say.
We started lovingly, ended shovingly.

2 Prescribed Non-Restrictions

The list is too short.
We could do everything on it
by Tuesday (this being Monday)
and then stare out the window
till Monday rolls round again.

Maybe we need new windows –
with better, longer views,
a different house, another town,
a new country, a foreign language
and face it, a longer list.

GUM: Genital-Urinary Medicine

3   Wish You Were Here

She hands me a little square of pale blue
paper roll, 'for dignity' she says.
I can cover up until the doctor comes.
My legs are floundering in the stirrups.

I hold this little square of pale blue
paper roll in front of the split
between my legs as my mind dredges
all ideas of dignity I have ever had.

Not one is strong enough.
At the same time, you are swimming
in the sea on the other side of the world
where blue sky covers all of you.

I hold this little square of pale blue
paper roll, in front of our continental rift.
I butterfly and breast stroke myself.
You can scissor kick yourself and crawl.

The Ticking Son

Every time the phone rings
I say to myself, 'that will be his mother'
and I rehearse what I'm going to say to her:

'Listen here, you with the funny Spanish name
who isn't really Spanish
married to the Jewish man
who isn't really Jewish – just a little.

You think you can phone me up
and in one Bob's-your-uncle phone call
find out what makes your son tick?

Listen, Mrs Chiquita-banana-mother –
that little *hijo* of yours is some
run-for-your-money man
who's had me on the run for years.

But I was hoping you'd ring.
There's stuff I want to talk about too,
like his sweet tooth and his sweet tongue,

his cocky way and his wayward cock,
his come-hither look and his slither come,
his fingers, those ten Tinkerbells
of wonderland, lighting all my lights.

What did you think your were doing –
you and that counterfeit husband of yours,
minting a new brand, irresistible man?

Do you think I ever thought of resisting?
Never! It was your darling boy
who buggered off into the sunset – schmunset.
You want to know what makes your son tick?

I'll tell you Cha Cha Mama! Hot Spanish spices,
chilli pepper slices – tango, salsa, samba
and bloody Leonard Cohen, slow enough to die from.'

Passing the Parcel

Passing the parcel back and forth between us,
dropping tears on the delicate tissue paper,
and crushing the ribbon with our sweaty hands,
has made the package nearly unrecognisable.

It might be a stage prop from a Christmas pantomime,
thrown from actor to actor in spurts, manhandled,
while the audience shouts, 'He's behind you!'
'Throw it!' So I look around, but you aren't.

It rattles like a nest of boxes, one inside the other
carefully disguised to look like something nice
which I could then hand to a friend, graciously.
Perhaps expensive chocolates are inside.

But I remember well what's in the inner box.
Why else would I be trying so hard to give it back?
It wasn't meant for me. It wasn't meant for me.
You are thinking to yourself exactly the same thing.

Passing the parcel back and forth between us,
we watch the damaged wrappings drop away,
we see the riddled ribbon undo itself like salty rope.
Believe me, there is no mistake boxed inside these boxes.

The Afternoon After

'In the afternoon after the morning
on which I loved you more
than I had ever loved you'...

that morning, part of the night before
which had come slowly, dawning
with the pink of our mouths

and getting full the way we did,
slotted into each other
and letting go, finally, to the light,

without ever sleeping in between
our midnight walk in the garden
and this wrapping and unwrapping

of sheets and limbs and eyelids
to wash each other's backs
and sort our scattered clothes,

we finally dressed and said goodbye
outside, under a net of mist
catching us first, then letting us go.

'In the afternoon after the morning
on which I loved you more
than I had ever loved you'...

is the beginning of a sentence
I can't bring myself to finish,
but you did. You did.

The Badly-Done-By Finish

There are certain scenes in any play
it would be good to avoid at the end.
You know – that one where the woman
doubles up and falls to the ground, sobbing
and everyone rushes over to help her?

'He's gone,' she says. 'I'll kill myself.'
And everyone crowds in, regardless,
greedily breathing as if there will never
be enough of what little air there is.
They hold her up since she's far too weak.

The end would be easier to direct
if everyone involved in the final scene
just walked off stage together, all pointing
in the same direction, all not stumbling,
all not speaking any final lines *at all*.

The Tin Dragon Fights Back

His golden feet got hot
and he had to be handled
with oven gloves. Do you
remember getting down
on your hands and knees
to scrape the melted wax
off the kitchen floor?

I could send him back to you
even though he won't fit
in a padded envelope.
I'd drive him to your place,
then singe open the jaws
of your letter box wide enough
to let his head poke through,

wondering at the same time
if I should ring the bell.
Fire breath and rumbling
might shake the door step under me
as I pull the snorting creature
closer into my chest, then firmly
straight through to my heart.

It will be hot inside the cavity
of my ribs, in between my lungs –
hot enough to sear that dark pink
dragon food – my only heart.
The chambers will quiver but
the blood will keep on pumping
until the organ cauterises itself.

Clutching a green tin dragon,
standing in front of your door,
I'm scorched, sizzled as a barbeque,
with my heart valves sealed
by some ridiculous trinket of love
which I'm trying to return in person,
but the dragon, fuck him, fights back.

My Friend Who Works

My friend who works in the wholefood store
said you came in to the shop today,
distracted, moving fast –
though the food itself around you
was whole and slow
and would be good for you –
eventually, good for you,
but it would take time.

Just a few things in a basket
over your arm, she told me –
not a big hibernation kind of shopping,
just a couple of brown paper packets
and some assorted jars.
She was at the other till and it was a busy time.

'Did he see you?' I asked.
'I don't think so,' she said.
'What kind of things did he get?' I asked
and she said 'I don't know.
The queues were too long –
I couldn't read the labels
but I noticed something
I'm sure you'll want to know.

He was by himself.
He's planning to get healthy alone.'
'Did he look well?' I asked.
'Do you think he'll succeed?'
'No,' said my friend who works in the wholefood store.
'He looked like shit.'

Scuffing

Life has scuffed the varnish off the kitchen floor
under the chair which is mine,
so we know whose life did it.

I had had higher goals all along
and this slipshod, half-cocked achievement
is not one of my valued successes.

First the varnish, then bits of the floor itself
have furred, feathered and flaked.
There's no shine left, no sheen, no preservative.

Call it a free-for-all at this point.
The sealed, now unsealed. The coated, disrobed.
Bare boards exposed and splintering.

How did it ever get this bad?
Could I have slid myself in and out
with less effect by trying harder to be softer?

I blame breakfast as well as lunch
and occasional cups of coffee with friends
and you for having left the table without asking.

Out of the Loop

You used to tell me about her,
when I was in and she was out.
I felt free to have opinions
about everything she did and said.

Now, you tell her about me,
since she is in and I am out.
She feels free to have opinions
about everything I do and say.

I do and say some pretty mean stuff
now that the loop is so tight –
the two of you bound up, knotted
and I'm not talked to, but about.

Now, out of your precious loop
I'm free to do and say what I please
to you and your lassoed lady.
Yank the rope. String her up.

Single Was Swell

Single was swell –
hell, I didn't wait
for calls, cars,
or handlebars.

Didn't give a shit –
didn't kit myself
in sexy knicks
watch skinflicks.

Single was swell –
well, calm, cool –
fool to fall
crack the pan,

hit the fire,
then expire
from the heat
your hand.

Single was swell –
hell! Now I'm charred
hard to handle
swindled, kindled.

Poetic Licence

Compared to Molly Peacock's man,
the poet's coals I am raking you over
are small potatoes, however, very hot.

He had to sit in the audience, smiling
while she told everyone exactly how
his scrotum looked. His in particular.

There is a much of a muchness,
surely, about all male private parts,
however she gave his a particular twist.

Could I pick them out in a line up?
Were they so accurately described
that I could name him in a locker room?

She didn't do badly, though I haven't yet
put her words to the test, nor his parts.
She mentioned a Baltimore Oriole's nest.

So, my love, what do my readers know
about you and your manhood which
you might have preferred to keep secret?

Piercings, size, stamina,
the odd taboo tattoo, studded parts,
a few erotic arts. Not much.

Molly Peacock, the American poet, said to her writing class, 'It is the job of women poets to describe men's bodies, every single bit of them.' And she did!

Early Train South

The shapes of winter trees move past,
frosted and only slightly greyer than the sky
which begins to bleach itself pink.
Everyone knows what trains can do to trees –
uproot them like the flicked pages of a book
fanned past the windows, whole landscapes in tow.

You were sitting in one of these trees,
cut out against the faint pink-and-blueing sky.
I had a glimpse of you, then you were gone.

You were holding a painted sign for me to read
but I couldn't make out all the words.
If memory serves, one of them was *forever*.

In spring, green will be spattered everywhere
and the clear cut shapes of the limbs will be gone.
If you make a sign then, I won't see it.

Graffiti

You say I take you higher and higher,
she drags you lower and lower. OK.

Let's put a red mark on the wall for *high*,
a black mark on the wall for *low*.

You can scribble your own stuff in between,
but then you'll have to choose – *me or her*.

You'll work it out, baby, come on!
Aim the cans! I'm high, she's low.

What a mess you're leaving behind.
You still can't choose?

Look around you!
You're not the only one confused.

Here Again

Here again? Is it possible,
exactly where the drawing pin
(a red one with a long plastic shank)
had pierced the spot before?

This place is really tender
from the last time it was punctured
and the pain of finding the spot
again has made me screw up my face.

I've had to close my eyes,
cover my head with my hands
and curl my body into a ball
so my belly is inside the curve.

This map with this mark is no good.
It shows the wrong place, this place.
Do you think we won't repeat the past?
Do you think we won't repeat the past?

Last Logging On

It's a Friday kind of thing
between signing off and signing on –
leaving the office and going home.

Do I mind that you think of me –
that you send me a message saying
I am beautiful?

The word beautiful makes me close my eyes
to remember what it was like. I can't imagine
who has sent this message, nor to whom,

though I know these people well
when they have nothing to say,
Monday to Thursday.

Hacker

You've cut me down
to a casual fling
by way of select and delete.

Keep it up and my love poems,
once lusty and lush, will be
only keyboard commands.

Launch. Enter. Control.
Open. Merge. Quit.

Dreaming Knows

By many deliberate acts of will
I have rearranged my inner city travel

to avoid the places you work and live.
I never pass them now.

I don't know if you're in or out, with her
or where your car is parked.

Even if I had to pass the end of your road,
I know I wouldn't look down.

I marvel at my control. Every waking hour
is determined, paced and curbed

though in my dreams I have your movements
clocked and mapped precisely.

Dreaming knows what bus you'll take
and which seat will be yours on the train.

Dreams hum the numbers into my ear
as I stand at the station in the ticket office queue.

Slow Pink

Everything is slower now.
Even the pink light seeping through
the new curtains dawdles on the sill.

I had wanted to change the room –
get rid of the old pink drapes,
but the cream-coloured cloth I bought
turned pink in spite of me
and nothing has really changed.

Dawn is just slower now –
rosier, shyer and more reluctant
than it ever was to come in.

In daylight, the new curtains
look like sheets of double cream, blushing,
pulled back against the climbing roses.
Anyone coming into the room
would be delighted by what they saw.

Why should I complain
about what is so obviously lovely
just because it was lovelier before?